Bullies,
Bigmouths
& So-called
Friends

J. Alexander

Hodder
Children's
Books

A division of Hachette Children's Books

Also by Jenny Alexander:

The Seven Day Bully-Buster
The Seven Day Brain Booster
The Seven Day Stress Buster
The Seven Day Self-esteem Super-booster

Acclaim for this book

'An important book for youngsters who want to become bulley-proof.'

Funday Times

'*Bullies, Bigmouths and So-called Friends* demonstrates that building up your self-esteem can help prevent bullying.'

ChildLine

'At last, a book that really helps you deal with the people in your life who are making you miserable ...'

The Bookseller

'Unique in teaching children how to boost their self-esteem and so prevent bullying from affecting their lives.'

Independent

There is much in this book that children might find of real help.'

Books For Keeps

Text copyright © Jenny Alexander 2003
Illustrations copyright © David Whittle 2003
Cover illustration © David Whittle 2003

Book design by Don Martin

Published in Great Britain in 2003
by Hodder Children's Books

A catalogue record for this book is available
from the British Library.

6

ISBN-13: 978 0 340 91184 6

Printed and bound by CPI Bookmarque Ltd, Croydon, Surrey

Hodder Children's Books
A division of Hachette Children's Books
338 Euston Road, London NW1 3BH
An Hachette UK Company
www.hachette.co.uk

Contents

1 Bullies, bigmouths, so-called friends... and you!

Bullies...

You know the type, they push you around, shut doors in your face, send you threatening text messages, take your dinner money, damage your things, mock you and make you look small.

Bigmouths...

You know the type. They make sarcastic comments about you, spread nasty rumours, bluejack you and say rude things behind your back.

So-called friends...

Aren't they the worst? They turn their back on you without saying why, tell everyone your secrets, block you on MSN and shut you out.

You...

Everyone gets hassle from bullies, bigmouths and so-called friends sometimes, but some people handle it better than others. How well do you handle it? Do the "Can you handle it?" quiz and find out.

Can you handle it?

Someone calls you a fat slob. Do you

1   Say it takes one to know one

2   Tell them to get lost

3   Tell them to get lost... and skip lunch

4   Go on a grapefruit diet

You're getting silent calls from an unknown number. Do you

1   Tell your phone company

2   Leave the line open and watch TV – it's their bill

3   Hang up and try to forget it

4   Plead with them to stop

Your friends shut you out and ignore you. Do you

1 Hang out with someone else

2 Try to be extra nice so they'll want you back

3 Decide never to speak to them again

4 Think no-one in the whole world likes you any more

Three members of the rugby team threaten to beat you up. Do you

1 Tell a teacher

2 Tell your big brother and his friends

3 Avoid them and hope they'll forget about it

4 Stop going to school

Some stroppy little kid kicks you. Do you

1 Say you'll hit him if he tries it again – and mean it

2 Say you'll hit him if he tries it again – and hope he doesn't

3 Laugh it off (it didn't hurt much anyway)

4 Run away

If you answered mostly 1...
Give this book to a jumble sale – go out and conquer the world!

If you answered mostly 2...
You can handle it, but read this book anyway because it's full of quizzes and stuff.

If you answered mostly 3...
You might not cope with bs, bs and s-c fs very well if you're feeling vulnerable, like when you've got problems at home. Read this book soon.

If you answered mostly 4...
Drop everything this minute and read on.

How to handle bullies, bigmouths and so-called friends... not!

People who seem quite sensible will often come out with surprisingly mad advice like...

'Just hit them back!'

This might be a good idea if you happen to be bigger and meaner than the person bashing you up, but how likely is that? Anyone who hits you is probably twice your size or part of a gang. Besides, most bullies, bigmouths and so-called friends don't hit you, so you can't hit them back anyway.

(If things get physical, tell a teacher. Schools are pretty good at dealing with physical bullying because they take it seriously, it's easy to investigate, and there's no question about who is in the wrong.)

'Pretend you don't care!'

Like anyone's going to be taken in!

(Unless, of course, you happen to be a world-class actor, in which case by all means give it a go.)

'Just ignore it!'

As if you wouldn't if you could...

'Avoid the places where bullies hang out'

Der! Like you aren't doing that already!

'Feel sorry for them – they're probably jealous of you, or having a hard time at home'

Worth a try if you're a saint, but what normal person is going to feel sorry for someone who's making their life a misery?

'Practise walking tall!'

It's pretty hard to look like a giraffe when all you really want to do is crawl under the nearest stone…

'Think of something witty to say'

Most likely outcome – you'll just give them something else to mock.

This kind of advice makes me cross. How can you act big and tough if you feel like a jelly? It's like saying to someone who's never been in a boxing ring, 'Put on the gloves, walk tall, pretend you aren't scared and go for a knock-out.'

That person is so going to get pasted!

How to handle bullies, bigmouths and so-called friends... yes, really!

Boxers prepare. They go to the gym and build up their fitness. They practise their skills. If you're in a bullies, bigmouths and so-called friends situation you can't just puff yourself up and look terrifying or they'll pop you like a balloon. You have to build up some solid self-confidence and courage. It takes time, but everyone can do it and it's well worth the effort.

The three little pigs

Three little pigs were sitting around cluttering the place up and their mum told them to get off their bottoms and build houses of their own. The first one got a bundle of straw and built a straw house; the second one got a bundle of sticks and built a stick house. Neither of them took more than ten minutes over it and they were pretty chuffed with themselves. They had a good laugh watching their brother slaving away building a proper house with bricks and mortar.

But then the big bad wolf comes sniffing round! One huff and puff and he's blown the house of straw down and gobbled up the first little pig. Ditto the house of sticks and the second little pig. But can he blow down the house of bricks? No! He can huff and puff till Christmas if he likes, but he still won't get to the third little pig.

And big bad bullies, bigmouths and so-called friends can't get to you either if you take the time to build up some good defences.

Boxers don't step into the ring until they believe they can win. If they look like a loser, they lose. Bullies, bigmouths and so-called friends can always spot a loser. Look at the line-up on the opposite page. If you wanted someone to pick on, which one would you choose: Sue, Tyrone, Annabel, Peter or Ben?

Sue Tyrone Annabel Peter

Ben

Now ask yourself, what makes Ben look like a loser? Is it because he's particularly ugly, puny, geeky, boffiny or stupid?

Ben looks like a loser because he feels like a loser. He can't defend himself because he's weighed down by bad thoughts.

I'm hopeless. Everyone hates me. I wish i was someone else.

Anyone can get bogged down by bad thoughts. Just look what happened to Ben.

Ben's story

Ben was bright, but not too bright. Good-looking, but not too good-looking. Sporty, but not David Beckham. He got on OK with everyone at school, had a couple of really good friends, and wouldn't have given two hoots if someone tried to pick on him, which they didn't. But then...

Ben and his family had to move to a different part of the country. Ben had lived in the South East all his life, and he thought it would be a great adventure living in the North. When he first walked into his new school, all the boys thought he looked cool and all the girls wanted to go out with him. But then...

He opened his mouth. Everyone laughed at the way he talked. They mimicked him. They called him

'posh'. Ben felt surprised and flustered. It had never occurred to him that he might not fit in.

Some of the kids really enjoyed seeing the new kid squirm (specially the boys, who were jealous). Every time he said anything, they mocked him, until he stopped saying anything at all. Which didn't help him to make new friends, as you can imagine.

Pretty soon, teasing Ben was just a habit for the kids in his new class. They didn't know it was really upsetting him because he never said. But it was. He got miserable and stopped wanting to go to school. **'Everyone hates me,'** he thought. **'I wish I was someone else'**...

There was nothing wrong with Ben. All the teasing would have been like water off a duck's back normally, but he was in a strange place a long way from all his friends. Bullies and bigmouths often make a beeline for kids who are vulnerable for some reason or another. And when you're vulnerable, bad thoughts can move in like a gang of squatters and make themselves at home.

Ben doesn't have to go on feeling like a loser: he just needs to change the way he thinks. Do "The traffic light test" to see if you do too.

The traffic light test

When people are horrible to me I often feel... (tick yes or no)

	Yes	No
'I don't want to talk about it'	☐	☐
'It's not my fault so there's nothing I can do about it'	☐	☐
'There must be something wrong with me'	☐	☐
'My whole life stinks'	☐	☐
'I'm not angry, I'm hurt'	☐	☐
'What if I can't deal with it?'	☐	☐

If you didn't have any 'Yes' ticks at all, you're on **green**. Go straight on thinking the way you do.

If you had one or two 'Yes' ticks, you're on **amber**. Go on thinking the way you do, but be ready to stop if things get worse.

If you had three or more 'Yes' ticks, you're on **red**. Stop and take a good look at the way you think. Change it before it makes a loser out of you!

2 'I don't want to talk about it'

If you don't want to talk about it you're probably thinking...

'I should be able to sort it out for myself.'

Well, talking about it is the best way to start!

Now you're probably saying, *'But there's nothing anyone else can do.'*

That's not the point! The point of talking about it is to make you

- feel better, because bad secrets make you uncomfortable and ashamed

- see the situation more clearly, because you can't see something you're sitting on

- act more calmly, because bottled-up feelings are like a shaken-up can of coke – lift the tab, and it goes off in your face

Science has shown that bottled-up feelings create unhealthy pressure in the body. Look at this diagram.

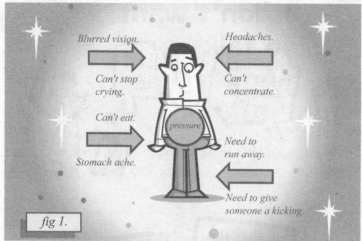

fig 1.

Now see what happens when you talk about things – the pressure is released.

fig 2.

Obviously, talking about things can have unwanted side-effects. You have to be careful who you tell, or any of these things can happen...

The safest way to start is by talking to someone who can't interfere. This is what we bulliesbigmouthsandso-calledfriendsologists call a **Step 1 Talkee**. Here are some examples: ChildLine, a diary, your rabbit, your favourite band, a chatroom, your finger buddy or even a friendly tree.

When you talk to your Step 1 Talkee you might be surprised how emotional you feel. Have a box of tissues handy. Have a pillow to punch! Releasing the pressure means it can all come gushing out at first.

Keeping a diary is a good idea anyway, even if you've got lots of other Step 1 Talkees. It helps you get things out of your system and see what's going on more clearly. It can be used as evidence too, along with any abusive text messages and emails, if you decide to tell your parents or teachers.

5 top tips for keeping a diary

1 Use an ordinary notebook, not a proper diary. Then on days when you feel like writing a lot you'll always have enough room, and when you don't feel like writing at all you won't have a gap.

2 Keep your diary somewhere safe. No-one should read it unless you want them to.

3 Write down the facts – dates, times, names and places.

4 Write down how you feel.

5 Be completely honest. Lying to your diary is like lying to yourself.

5 top tips for keeping a picture diary

If you don't like writing, you can keep a picture diary.

1 **Write the date.**

2 **Draw yourself.** It doesn't have to look like you – if you're feeling grumpy you could draw a hippopotamus, or if you're bright and cheerful you could draw a flower. You could draw yourself as a man, woman or child, with short black hair or long blonde hair, in fancy clothes or rags...

3 **Put other people in if you want to.** They don't have to look like themselves either.

4 **Fill in some background** with anything that feels right, maybe houses or trees, a street or a desert, a room or a black hole.

Writing a diary can help you to get things off your chest when you are having a hard time. One of the most famous diarists of all times, Anne Frank, said the best thing about her diary was that she could write her thoughts and feelings in it – *'otherwise, I'd absolutely suffocate,'* she said.

Millions of people have read Anne Frank's diary. Nelson Mandela read it when he was in prison in South Africa, and he said it gave him great encouragement. Most of us have never been so oppressed, but Anne Frank's diary can help us understand what it must be like.

A lot of bullies, bigmouths and so-called friends don't understand how it feels to be picked on and pushed around. When they find out, it can come as quite a shock. Amanda used her diary as a Step 1 Talkee when two girls in her class started picking on her. Eventually, she plucked up the courage to tell her head teacher. She took her diary with her.

Amanda's story

Amanda lived with her mum, and when her mum got ill, Amanda had to stay with foster parents for a while. Her foster parents were nice, but Amanda missed her mum and felt worried about her all the time.

Jan and Charlene thought it was witty and amusing to call Amanda 'cuckoo'. You work it out. They made cuckoo calls whenever they passed her in the corridors.

Amanda wrote everything down in her diary, how many times each day, each lesson, they teased her. She wrote about how lonely and terrified she felt, with her mother in hospital and her classmates turning against her. When her head teacher read the diary, she had to reach for a tissue!

The head teacher, with Amanda's permission, called Jan and Charlene to her office and read them a bit of Amanda's diary. Jan and Charlene were shocked. They were ashamed of themselves. They had not thought about Amanda's feelings at all. **'We were just having a laugh,'** they said.

The teasing stopped straight away. Amanda's classmates started to be much more supportive, and they were delighted for her when her mum was finally well enough to come home.

A head teacher is a **Step 2 Talkee**. Once you've got things off your chest by talking to a Step 1 Talkee you'll be feeling calmer. Then you might decide, like Amanda, that you're ready to go on to Step 2.

All the Step 2 Talkees could interfere. If that's what you want, say so. Don't be afraid to ask for help or advice. If that isn't what you want, say that too. Be clear. Say, *'I just want to talk to you about something that's bothering me. I don't need any help or advice at the moment, but if I do later, I will ask.'*

Here are some examples of great Step 2 Talkees: your Mum, Dad, brother, sister, Gran, Grandpa, teacher, friend, school counsellor.

If you do ask any of these guys for help and advice there's obviously a chance they won't come up with anything useful. But once you've told, it's much easier to tell again, and keep going until someone does. When it comes to telling, the first time is the worst. Check out Stella's story.

Stella's story

Stella hated going on the school bus (who doesn't? It's horrible!). The big girls at the back shouted rude things and threw crisps at her. Stella told her mum, and her mum said, **'Take no notice.'**

It got harder to take no notice when the big girls snatched Stella's bag and emptied it on the floor. They threw her things all over the bus. Stella told her teacher. She would rather have juggled porcupines, but it felt like

she had no choice. She couldn't sort out the big girls on her own.

Stella's teacher told the big girls to stop. That afternoon, they grabbed Stella's bag and spat in it. They threatened to set their brothers on Stella if she told again. Stella told again.

This time she told her head of year, Mr Malloy. She also told him her teacher had only made things worse. Mr Malloy talked to the big girls. He said he was sure they were just having a bit of fun, but Stella was really upset. He didn't think they were the kind of people who would want to pick on a girl several years younger than them who was all on her own.

Mr Malloy told Stella the girls wanted to talk to her. She was quaking in her trainers! He went off and left them alone together. The big girls said sorry to Stella. **'We were just having a laugh,'** they said. **'We didn't know you were upset.'**

Obviously, all 3 girls knew that wasn't true, but it gave them a way to get out of the situation with no-one losing face. Clever Mr Malloy! He could have threatened the big girls with all kinds of sanctions – even the police (you can't go around threatening people with violence). Probably he would have, if his first strategy didn't work. Probably they knew that.

They also knew that Stella would not keep their nasty little games a secret, because she had shown she would tell and keep telling if needs be. They never bullied her again. They bullied Petra instead, but that's another story.

Petra's story

Petra didn't tell anyone when two big girls started bullying her. They pushed her in the playground and kicked her in the corridors. They

called her names. The longer it went on the worse it got.

Petra pretended she was ill so she wouldn't have to go to school. Her mum took her to the doctor. The doctor said the commonest cause of headaches and stomach aches in kids was bullying at school. He told Petra's mum that an awful lot of his young patients had been off school with headaches and stomach aches lately.

Petra's mum wrote a letter to someone on the school council. She asked if the school could have a bully box.

The bully box gave everyone a chance to tell without having to give their names, and pretty soon the teachers saw that a certain two big girls were making life miserable for a lot of younger ones.

The big girls were given the choice between seeing the school counsellor to sort out their behaviour or getting their parents involved. One of them

had parents who would be angry and abusive (bullies often have bullying parents) and the other had parents who would be disappointed (they thought the sun shone out of her, and she could do no wrong).

They're seeing the counsellor!

You've got nothing to lose by talking about bullies, bigmouths and so-called friends. Talking will make you feel better even if you don't want any help and advice. It will help you to see things more clearly and work out what you want to do.

You might decide you can deal with the situation yourself. You might want your teacher to help you without letting anyone know you have told, by letting you sit further away from your bs, bs and s-c fs for example, or doing PE in a different group. You might decide to tell more openly, and send a clear message to the you-know-whats that you aren't going to take it lying down.

'I don't want to talk about it' is a loser attitude. Get rid of it. Start talking!

3 'It's not my fault so there's nothing I can do about it'

'It's not my fault so there's nothing I can do about it,' means *'If people would just stop being nasty to me, I'd be fine.'* So what's your plan? Sit around and wait for them to stop? You could be waiting for a long time.

'It's not my fault so there's nothing I can do about it,' means *'I shouldn't have to do anything about it!'*

OK, so you shouldn't have to deal with bullies, bigmouths and so-called friends, but sometimes you just do. It's called getting real.

GET REAL!

Cut this out and put it on your wall.

If you're borrowing this book, you'd better copy it out instead.

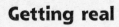

Getting real

In fantasy land, people are always nice to each other. In the real world, people can be cruel. You can't change how other people behave. But you can change how you respond. The ability to choose how you respond is response-ability. Taking responsibility for yourself means you don't have to be helpless any more.

Here's Leanne being a bigmouth, and Julie not handling it.

I wish I had a coat like that.

Here's Leanne being a bigmouth again, and Julie choosing a different way to respond.

In the first instance, Julie blamed Leanne for making her unhappy. But the second set of pictures shows she didn't have to let Leanne make her unhappy at all. People can say horrible things to you, but you don't have to let it get to you. Blaming other people for your unhappiness won't make you happy. It will actually keep you unhappy. Who wants to be unhappy? Let go of blame right now!

Letting go of blame

Try these three easy techniques for letting go of blame. You can practise them at home or at school, because you'll find – once you start noticing – that everyone's busy blaming other people most of the time!

1 Not you... me

Your feelings are your own. Whenever you find yourself thinking *'You made me angry... you frightened me... you upset me'*, switch from you to me. Say, *'I let myself get angry... I let you frighten me... I let you upset me.'*

But don't beat yourself up about it. We all let other people get to us sometimes. Just acknowledge it and let it go.

2 The 'f' word and the 'b' word

Never use the 'f' word and the 'b' word (which, as everyone knows, are 'fault' and 'blame').

Also, cut down on the 'sh' word (no, not that one! The other 'sh' word – 'should'). Whenever you can, use 'could' instead because it feels much better. For example,
'I should've done better' is like a final judgement, but *'I could've done better'* opens up other possibilities.

3 Think hot potatoes!

When someone is nasty to you, think of their nastiness as a hot potato they're giving to you. If you hold on to it you'll hurt your hands. So give it back.

Giving back the hot potato isn't about retaliation – it's about refusing to let people dump their nastiness on you.

That was Will taking the hot potato (notice, he's blaming his mum!). But he could just give it back…

Taking a no-blame approach when it comes to bullies, bigmouths and so-called friends is hard because it feels like you're letting them off the hook – which they certainly don't deserve. But the only person who suffers when you are eaten up by blame and righteous indignation is yourself. When you let go of blame, the person you're actually letting off the hook is you.

So start with easy situations like your annoying kid sister or irritating Uncle Jack. Experience how the whole blame-and-fault thing stops you sorting things out in other areas of your life before you try to let go of blame in the bs, bs and s-c fs situation.

Notice how, whenever something goes wrong, we immediately look for someone to blame. If someone breaks a plate it's all, *'You shouldn't have left it there!'*, *'I was in a rush because of your piano lesson'*, *'I told Mum those stupid plates were a bad buy!'* None of which is going to bring the plate back.

Blaming the bs, bs and s-c fs isn't going to bring your happiness back either. You have to do that for yourself, like Darren did.

Darren's story – 1

Darren's sister Louise was bossy and horrible to him. Their parents thought it was just a stage she was going through, so they didn't do anything about it.

Darren got really fed up with Louise having a go. It made him feel miserable. Why was she so horrible to him? She was his sister! She was supposed to be nice!

One day Louise did something so spiteful, Darren was actually shocked. He suddenly realised that it didn't make any difference how she was supposed to be; the fact was, she was horrible. It was no good waiting for her to be nice; he would just have to stop letting her nastiness get to him instead.

That night, there was a programme on TV called, **'Happiness is the best revenge!'** Darren grinned. He wrote it on a piece of paper so he wouldn't forget it.

You know what to do!

Letting go of guilt

Most bullies, bigmouths and so-called friends are brilliant at playing the blame game. They'll give you a kicking and say you asked for it. They'll shout abuse at you and say you brought it on yourself. They'll say things like, *'You made me do that... you shouldn't be so annoying... you should keep out of my way.'*

Of course, they're bang out of order. But it can be easy to fall into the trap of believing them. After all, why should anyone want to hurt you if you haven't done anything to deserve it? The only logical explanation is that you must have done something – you just don't know what.

The great thing is that when you let go of blame, you also let go of guilt. As soon as you see it's your choice how you respond to other people, you also see it's their choice how they respond to you. Other people's aggressiveness is never your fault – it's their responsibility.

Darren's story – 2

'Get over yourself!' Louise used to snap at Darren when she'd managed to reduce him to a quivering wreck. But she didn't like it much when he did.

Although it didn't bother him so much any more, Darren couldn't help thinking he must be doing something wrong, or else Louise would leave him alone – perhaps he really was so stupid and annoying she couldn't help hating him.

But then he thought it through. If he could stop getting upset when she had a go at him, then she could stop having a go, couldn't she, even if she felt provoked?

Now if she tries that old 'You made me lose my temper' thing, Darren just shrugs it off. **'Get over yourself!'** he says.

If you think you shouldn't have to deal with other people's nastiness, you're right. But the thing is, would you rather be right, or happy?

If you want to be happy, don't just say, *'It's not my fault so there's nothing I can do about it.'* Take response-ability. Say, *'It's not my fault – but I can deal with it.'*

4 'There must be something wrong with me'

This is exactly what bullies, bigmouths and so-called friends want you to think, and there aren't many people who could stand up to lots of teasing and abuse without starting to wonder.

In the last major ChildLine survey, 52 per cent of children who admitted bullying others said they did it because they felt angry or jealous, and 30 per cent because they were bored or thought it was funny. None of them mentioned their victims' characteristics at all.

The golden rule with teasing and bullying is

Don't take it personally.

DON'T TAKE IT PERSONALLY

Cut this out and put it on your wall.
Use blutak, not cellotape

Here are three great ways to build up your self-confidence and help you not to take things personally –

1 Accept yourself

2 Be nice to yourself

3 Enjoy being you

1 Accept yourself

The first thing to get to grips with is this –

You are not perfect!

In fact, nobody's perfect (come to think of it, copy that out and stick it on your wall, as well). Nobody has a perfect body, mind, or personality. Not being perfect is part of the human condition – if we were perfect we'd be angels. If we were already perfect we couldn't learn and grow.

'I know I'm not perfect,' I hear you say, *'that's the whole problem!'* Don't get your knickers in a knot... I didn't say *know* you aren't perfect – I said *accept* it. Accept it and enjoy it – because not having to be perfect means you don't have to be hurt by criticism.

And another thing – we all make mistakes. *'To err is human,'* as Shakespeare said. Accept your mistakes and move on.

The second thing to get to grips with is this –

You are not all bad, either!

Nobody's perfect, but everybody has their strengths. The boy who played like a donkey on the football pitch performed like Einstein in his maths exam, for example. There are two sides to every coin. Do this little exercise, and you might find out something interesting about the two sides of you.

The two sides of you

You will need a pencil and paper

Method

1   Draw a line down the middle of the paper from top to bottom.

2   On the left side of the line list six good things about yourself. Don't be modest and don't spend long on it – just write the first things that come into your head.

3   On the right side of the line list six bad things about yourself.

4   Study the two lists carefully.

Does anything strike you about them? No? OK, then do the same for your best friend and your worst enemy. Can you spot anything now?

Look at the lists I made for myself. I've put them in order. Can you see a pattern?

Good things about me	Bad things about me
I'm truthful	I can be tactless
I'm a good leader	I'm bossy
I've got a great imagination	I'm no good at practical things
I'm quite caring	I can be over-sensitive
I like my own company	I'm not a team player
I'm not afraid to do my own thing	I can be selfish

The things I like about myself are just different aspects of the things I hate. Being a good leader means most of the time I have the energy and confidence to help people sort things out... but sometimes I don't get it right, and they think I'm just a bossy-boots.

Now have another look at your lists. Do any of the things you like about yourself match up with the things you don't? If not, think about the things you dislike about yourself. They may be the negative side of great qualities you haven't noticed in yourself before.

Accept your weaknesses and your strengths, because you can't have one without the other.

The sad case of Dr Jekyll and Mr Hyde

Dr Jekyll was a respectable doctor whose only dream was to be a fine upstanding member of the community. Unfortunately, he also liked boozing and letting his hair down, which he took to doing in secret.

Dr Jekyll didn't want his wild side ruining his reputation, so he invented a potion that could split the two sides of himself into two different people. The good side looked just like respectable Dr Jekyll, tall and smart, and the bad side was small and evil-looking, with very hairy hands. He called the bad side Mr Hyde.

When Dr Jekyll wanted to go out on the town, he drank the potion and became Mr Hyde; when he'd had enough of partying, he drank some more potion and turned back into Dr Jekyll. For a time, things went well, with Dr Jekyll having his cake, as it were, and Mr Hyde eating it.

But you can't disown your bad side forever (that's the moral of the story) and one day Dr Jekyll drank the potion, became Mr Hyde and got stuck! He couldn't change back! Then he had to face the consequences of all Mr Hyde's evil-doing, and he decided to kill himself rather than go to the gallows.

(This is not a true story, in case you're wondering. It was made up by Robert Louis Stevenson.)

Sour grapes

Some people are picked on for their weaknesses – for being shy, or clumsy or slow to learn, for example. Others are picked on for their strengths. People who are particularly brilliant, attractive, lucky or brave often have problems with bullies, bigmouths and so-called friends.

I read in the paper about a girl who was teased because the press hailed her as a heroine for saving her sister's life. After months of teasing, that girl killed herself. Her story makes me very angry and sad.

When people pick on others who are richer, nicer, cleverer, prettier, better at sports than they are, it's called **sour grapes**. Don't accept sour grapes from anyone. Let bullies, bigmouths and so-called friends go and choke on them!

That's what Jonny did...

Jonny's story

Jonny was brilliant at school work and he always came top in tests. All the teachers thought he was amazing, and all the kids called him a boffin. But it was quite good humoured.

Then along came SATs. Aaaaarghh...! Everyone started to get really stressy. Some of the teasing got nasty. Jonny was fed up. He decided to stop coming top, so the other kids would get off his back. He tried to do badly in a science test, and managed to come third. Would it be enough?

When the teacher gave out the results they were all stunned. Nobody said a thing. But at the next break time the kids started teasing Jonny again – for not coming top!

Being so bright, Jonny soon worked out that they were going to tease him whatever he did. He decided he might as well go back to coming top all the time. If the other kids didn't like it, too bad!

2   Be nice to yourself

(I love the word 'nice' because teachers always say you mustn't use it. That's me doing my own thing!)

First of all, see how nice you are by doing the "How nice are you?" quiz.

How nice are you?

Your friend is upset because Mr Sarcastic the science teacher has had a go at him. Do you

1   Laugh

2   Tell him he's stupid for getting upset

3   Say Mr Sarcastic's a prat

4   Suggest a game of cards at break time to take his mind off it

Your friend's off school with a broken leg because someone has pushed her off her bike. Do you

1   Stop being friends with her (you don't want to get pushed off yours)

2   Say it's her own fault for having such a flash bike

3   Send her a get well card

4   Call round with a box of chocs

Some older kids have put your friend's shoe down the toilet and run off. Do you

1   Pull the flush

2   Ask what he did to wind them up

3   Say they're just idiots

4   Take it out and rinse it under the tap

One of your friends is being shut out by the rest of your group. Do you

1   Join in rejecting her

2   Join in, but tell her privately you don't mean it

3   Try not to get involved

4   Stay friends (and let those losers do what they like!)

Mostly 1...
   You're as nice as a deadly virus.

Mostly 2...
   You're as nice as Mr Sarcastic the science teacher.

Mostly 3...
   You're as nice as pie.

Mostly 4...
   You're as nice as pie, chips and peas!

I'm guessing you mostly answered 3 or 4 because most people are nice (and did you know, it's scientifically proven that people who get picked on tend to be unusually nice?).

Now try this quiz to find out how nice you are to yourself.

How nice are you to yourself?

You are upset because Mr Sarcastic the science teacher has had a go at you. Do you

1 Feel he's right to mock you

2 Hate yourself for getting upset

3 Think Mr Sarcastic's a prat

4 Decide to cheer yourself up with a game of cards later

You're off school with a broken leg because someone has pushed you off your bike. Do you

1   Wish you were somebody else (bad things always happen to you)

2   Think it's your own fault for having such a flash bike

3   Hope to feel better soon

4   Cheer yourself up with a big box of chocs

Some older kids have put your shoe down the toilet and run off. Do you

1   Want to flush your whole life down the drain

2   Think you must've done something to deserve it

3   Say they're just idiots

4   Take it out and wash it

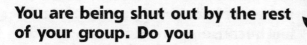

You are being shut out by the rest of your group. Do you

1 Reject yourself ('I wish I was someone else...')

2 Wish you were someone else if that would get you back in – but actually still think you're OK

3 Try to take no notice

4 Do your own thing and let those losers get on with it

You might have noticed that this quiz is spookily similar to the first one.

If you didn't get mostly 3s and 4s this time, what's going on? How come you're nice to your friends, but not very nice to yourself?

Be your own best friend

When bullies, bigmouths and so-called friends are having a go at you, imagine what you would think and feel if it was happening to a friend instead. Then it will be easier for you to see what's really going on, and be much nicer to yourself.

Being a loyal friend means tolerating someone's faults and forgiving their mistakes. It means sticking by them when they're having a hard time. Having a loyal friend makes you feel safe in the world, more confident and relaxed.

But friends come and go. There's only one person who will definitely be there forever, and that's you. If you can learn to be your own best friend, you'll have a friend for life.

3 Enjoy being you

Everyone's different – so you could say we're all the same!

But being different can feel dangerous. Most people want to fit in, and not stand out in the crowd.

If you happen to love the same clothes, music and activities as other people your age, then there's no problem. But if you don't, trying to fit in is like trying to squeeze your foot into a shoe that's three sizes too small – even if you manage it, you won't get far and it'll hurt like hell.

It's the same if your mum wants you to take up playing the cello because she loves it and thinks you will too. Or if your dad wants you to take up kick boxing because he reckons it'll build up your strength and confidence. If you don't really want to, it isn't going to work.

You can't enjoy being you if you don't do what you enjoy. If you love lace-making or birdwatching, if you're a trainspotter or a computer nerd – go for it! (Of course, you might decide not to tell the bs, bs and s-c fs what you do in your spare time – but don't let that put you off doing it.)

The same thing applies to how you feel as well as what you do. If you love eating meat like all your friends, for example, there's no problem. But if you're a vegetarian you probably feel very differently about the whole meat thing.

If your mum loves slushy romances, if your dad hates cats, you won't necessarily feel the same. Nobody can tell you what to feel. Nobody can know what you feel either, unless you tell them.

Trying to feel the same way as other people is going to have you hobbling along in the too-small shoe again. Don't disown your feelings. You may not necessarily want to express them all the time...

...but they are yours, you're entitled to them, and accepting them is an important part of enjoying being you.

When you find it hard enjoying being you, try making this "Quick pick-me-up pic" (don't worry – you don't have to be Van Gogh to do it!)

The quick pick-me-up pic

You will need

- some old magazines
- some scissors
- a glue stick
- a large sheet of paper (or stick two smaller sheets together – the join won't show)
- a clock or watch

Method

1 Give yourself five minutes to flick through the magazines, tearing out anything that appeals to you. Include words, whole pictures, bits of pictures, patches of colour or pattern.

2 Spread the images you have torn out on the floor. They won't all fit on your sheet of paper. Select the ones you like best, tearing or cutting them down to size. Stick them on to your sheet of paper. Don't think about it. Don't take more than ten minutes altogether.

The "Quick pick-me-up pic" is a picture of things you like – colours, textures, patterns, places, creatures, activities, people. Stick it on your wall and enjoy it. Now you are enjoying being you!

If you think there's something wrong with you, there is – it's that you think there's something wrong with you! Bullies, bigmouths and so-called friends don't need a reason for being horrible to you – they need an excuse. If you change whatever it is they're teasing you for (get a new bag... stop chewing your nails... do badly in tests) they'll just find something else to criticise.

Accept yourself, be nice to yourself, and enjoy being you... you're OK.

5 'My whole life stinks'

The technical term for this attitude is *'throwing the baby out with the bath water.'* It's when you let your whole life go down the plug-hole because part of it isn't working.

The problem is that if you let the bad stuff get to you, you stop even noticing the good. Try "The blue game" to see how it works.

The blue game

Take a long look around the room, noticing all the things that are blue. Don't turn the page until you think you've got them all.

Now close your eyes and try to remember all the things you saw that were green.

Hard, isn't it? "The blue game" shows that you only notice what you're actually looking at. Focusing on bad stuff like bullies, bigmouths and so-called friends can make you stop noticing the good things in your life. But it also works the other way round – focusing on the good stuff can make you stop noticing the bad.

Pollyanna and the glad game

Pollyanna had her own way of focusing on the good stuff which she called 'the glad game'. Whatever happened to her, she said **'I'm glad!'**, even if it was something terrible. Then she would start looking for all the reasons why she could be glad.

Pollyanna had a major challenge with the glad game because an awful lot of bad things happened to her. Her beloved father died, all her clothes and toys were given away and she was sent to live with a nasty aunt, to name but a few. Then lots of people were horrible to her before she finally got run over and couldn't walk any more...

Obviously, Pollyanna is one of the most irritating heroines you could imagine, and we call people who are annoyingly jolly all the time 'Pollyannas' after her. But millions of people have read the book because Pollyanna's method is so interesting.... and it works.

Check it out in *Pollyanna* by Eleanor H. Porter.

Here's a four-point plan to help you focus on the good things in life.

1 Think positive

A lot of people think you should always expect the worst because then you won't get disappointed if it happens, or you'll be more ready to deal with it. But actually expecting the worst is a real loser attitude. It wears you down with worry and unhappiness.

Instead you should expect the best.

EXPECT THE BEST

You know what to do!

Expecting the worst won't stop you feeling disappointed if it happens, and it won't help you deal with it because you'll be such a shivering wreck of nerves by then! Plus, of course, if it doesn't happen, you'll feel like a right idiot... Like Steven.

Steven's story

Steven had to give a talk on something great that had happened to him when he was small. He called his talk, 'When my dad won a medal in the Olympic Games'. He took the medal to school as a visual aid. At dinner time, he left it in the classroom. Then he thought that wasn't a good idea, so he went back to get it... but the medal was gone!

Steven went into a panic. What if someone had stolen it? What if it had fallen down a drain? What if it had got thrown away? He searched the whole classroom, then went to get his friends to help him search again.

They didn't find it, but they said, **'Don't get into a state. It's bound to show up.'** Steven was too busy having a nervous breakdown to listen.

By the end of dinner time, Steven was in a complete state. How was he going to tell his dad he had lost his precious medal? Then the teacher breezed in, took the medal out of her bag and put it on the table. Ten seconds before Steven went back to the classroom to get it, his teacher had had the same idea. She had taken it to the staffroom for safe keeping.

Oh, Steven! Was that embarrassing, or what?

Expecting the best means you feel happy and confident most of the time, because most of the time not much happens at all. Come the catastrophe, you're stronger and more able to deal with it. (If you expect the best the catastrophe is actually less likely to happen – yes, that's a scientific fact!)

You can develop a positive mental attitude by using affirmations.

Affirmations

Affirmations are things you say to yourself, and they act like conditioning – your brain absorbs and believes them on an unconscious level, even if you can't really believe them yourself.

To make an affirmation, first ask yourself, *'What do I want?'*

For example – *'I want this book to be a bestseller.'*

Now say what you want as if it has already happened. Start with, *'Right now...'*

For example – *'Right now, this book is a bestseller!'*

'Right now, this book is a bestseller' is a great affirmation for me. If I write it out and put it on

my wall, use it as a bookmark, repeat it several times before I start work each day, it will make me feel happy and confident. Then I'll write better and be more likely to have a bestseller.

Always use positive words in affirmations and avoid negative ones like 'can't', 'aren't' or 'isn't'. *'Right now, my so-called friend Helen isn't being horrible to me'* is nowhere near as powerful as *'Right now, Helen really likes me!'*

Affirmations work because they open you up to the possibility of having what you want. Even an affirmation like, *'Right now, I am incredibly rich!'* can work, in the sense that you can't be rich unless you believe you can, and know you want it. As Henry Ford the car maker once said –

'If you believe you can or you can't – you're right!'

You can have several affirmations on the go at the same time. Write them out and put them somewhere you'll notice them. Repeat each one twelve times when you wake up and twelve times when you go to bed. As you repeat them, feel the feelings as if what you want is happening right now. Experience in your imagination the joy and triumph of having what you want, because that's the first step towards getting it.

2 Talk Positive

Can't, mustn't, won't, don't, shouldn't…
Difficult, impossible, never…

Try going for one whole hour without using any
negative words. (Do I hear you say, *'I can't…
It's too difficult… I don't want to'?!*)

Noticing how many negative words you use is a
way of spotting your own negative thinking.
Changing the words, changes the thinking.
(Say, *'OK, I'll give it a go!'*)

Try making a good/bad day diary to get the feel
of it.

The good/bad day diary

1   When you get home from school, write
one page about your day.

2   Put a ring round all the negative
words.

3   Now write another page about your
day, without using any negative words.

You'll have to change what you mention, and think positive.

I didn't go on the bus because it's horrible we had Science first thing and I couldn't do it There weren't any chips left at lunch and the pizza wasn't very nice.

I walked to school. We had a Science test and then did drama. I had pizza for lunch, and I was still hungry so I got two donuts for pudding...

3   Feel positive

Positive emotions make you stronger and
healthier as well as happier – that's a fact.
Lots of experiments have shown that bad
feelings make you weak and good feelings make
you strong.

The best feeling of all is love, and you don't need
anyone else to help you experience it. Try this
experiment.

Look around the room and choose something you
have no feelings about at all, for example a coffee
table. Look at it for a while. Think to yourself, *'I
love you, coffee table.'* (OK, I know it's mad, but
bear with me.)

Now say out loud, *'I love you, coffee table!'*

Even loving a coffee table can make you smile and
feel happy, though a coffee table can't love you
back. It's your own love energy that you feel,
being reflected back to you. The more you love,
the more you feel loved, and the stronger,
healthier and happier you become.

That's why loving your enemy is the ultimate
victory – whether he likes it or not, you are taking
power from him (however, that's only for the
advanced student).

Here's April in the English Corridor, a famous no-go area she has to go through every day.

If you were Big Brian the class Bully walking past, what would you do?

Now here's April getting some positive love energy.

Do you still absolutely have to kick her bag?

The other big-league positive feeling is gratitude. Experiments have shown that gratitude is a better painkiller than pills! Plus it's brilliant at helping you notice the good stuff in your life. Start every day by saying thank you for all the things you like...

4 Act positive

The things you do every day have a big impact on how you feel. For example, exercise makes you feel happier, not just when you're doing it but for the rest of the day. A half hour walk every day has the same effect on your serotonin level (happiness chemicals in the brain) as taking anti-depressant drugs.

You don't have to be a world-class sprinter or athlete. Kicking a ball against a wall, wandering round the shops, taking the dog for a walk, running up and down the stairs a few times – they're all great ways to bump up your serotonin.

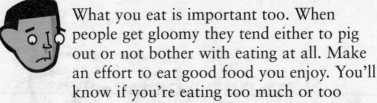

What you eat is important too. When people get gloomy they tend either to pig out or not bother with eating at all. Make an effort to eat good food you enjoy. You'll know if you're eating too much or too little because your stomach will soon start complaining. If your stomach is happy, so are you.

Last but not least – in fact, most important of all – check your TV habits. If you watch lots of programmes about wars, crimes and horrible illnesses – including the News – that is definitely not going to help you feel cheerful. Switch over! Choose adventures and comedy programmes. Laughing is a top tonic – it actually boosts your immune system. Plus it makes you feel much more positive about life.

Hold on to the good things in your life because you need them to help you get through the bad. Think, talk, feel and act positive (copy out, stick up!). Pull the plug on the dirty water – but hold on to the baby!

6 'I'm not angry – I'm hurt'

Just to recap...

bullies are those charming people who push you around, shut doors in your face, pin you against the wall, threaten you, take your dinner money, mock you and make you look small...

bigmouths are those lovely individuals who make sarcastic comments about you, spread nasty rumours and say rude things behind your back...

so-called friends are people you trust who turn their back on you without saying why, tell everyone your secrets and shut you out.

If they don't make you feel angry, they should!

Mad Mick, 'Six Pack' Parsons and the flying school bag

Try this experiment. Imagine Mad Mick and 'Six Pack' Parsons have taken your school bag and chucked it over the fence, and now they've run off laughing. The bag's lying in the road; you're standing looking at it through the wire. You're feeling confused. Why should they be so horrible to you? What've you ever done to them? You're hurt and bewildered.

Shut your eyes and really imagine it. Check out how your body feels. What does it want to do?

Now imagine the whole thing again. Mad Mick and 'Six Pack' Parsons have taken your school bag and chucked it over the fence, and now they've run off laughing. The bag's lying in the road; you're standing looking at it through the wire. You're feeling furious! How dare they be so horrible to you? What've you ever done to them? You're hopping mad!

Shut your eyes and really imagine it. How does your body feel now? What does it want to do?

When you feel hurt and upset, your energy drops. You feel helpless, and all you want to do is curl up in a hole. When you feel angry, you're bursting with energy. You could rip up trees, sprint for Britain and tackle tigers!

Feeling angry is good news when you fall foul of bullies, bigmouths and so-called friends, because anger is energy, and you need energy to defend yourself. Anger is like fire – you can be inflamed by anger, have a fiery temper, get hot under the collar, have a heated discussion or a blazing row. Anger can flare up and boil over. Like fire, anger can warm and energise you but if you don't know how to use it safely it can be dangerous.

That's why a lot of people are afraid of getting angry. They change it into something else. They say they're hurt, fed up, disappointed, depressed, bored, amazed, concerned, anxious... Some people will even tell you they never feel angry at all.

You can learn how to handle anger safely. Do this quiz to find out whether you need some tips... or are you already A+ at anger?

Are you A+ at anger?

That spiteful type Marie calls you a boffin as you all file in for a science test. Do you

1   Get angry and smack her stupid face

2   Get angry and come top in the test

3   Get angry and smack Julia (she sniggered and she's smaller than you)

4   Cry

Two boys from the other team push you over in a football match. Do you

1   Get angry and push them back

2   Get angry and score a goal

3   Get angry and push their weedy sweeper

4   Go off injured

Your best CD's got scratched. Do you

1   Get angry and bash your brother up (he probably did it)

2   Get angry and find out how it happened

3   Get angry and shout at your little sister

4   Go to your room and sulk

Your so-called friend tells everyone in the music lesson that you write soppy songs in your spare time. Do you

1   Get angry and bash her over the head with a cymbal

2   Get angry and write a brilliant song

3   Get angry and make life hard for the teacher (he's new and nervous)

4   Feel ill and have to go to the sick bay

If you answered mostly 1...

> **D–** You're a danger to yourself and everybody else!

If you answered mostly 2...

> **A+** Go to the top of the class, and skip the rest of this chapter.

If you answered mostly 3...

> **C** You're a danger to other people and probably not too proud of yourself.

If you answered mostly 4...

> **B–** On the up side, no-one else gets hurt. On the down side, you might as well lie on the ground under a big sign saying *'Please walk all over me'*.

So, all you people who could do better – let's talk about anger!

Anger is not the same as aggression

Aggression...

is turning your anger against other people in order to hurt them, get revenge, or force them to do what you want them to do. Shouting and swearing at people, making threats, and being violent are all aggressive acts.

Anger...

is the power to know what you want and what you don't want. It's the energy to work towards getting it.

Here's Iris. She's really angry about people letting their dogs foul the pavement where she lives. She shouts at them...

She threatens them...

Iris's neighbour, George, is angry about all the dogs' mess in the street, too. He expresses his views in a letter to the local paper...

Dear Sir, I am writing to ask your readers whether other people are concerned as i am about the problem of dogs' mess on our street.

He organises a meeting...

Join the "Clean up our village Campaign!"

Village ·Hall·

Iris got angry and aggressive – what did she achieve? George got angry and used his anger to show him what he wanted (*'I want to be able to go for a walk without having to look at the pavement all the time'*) and give him the energy to go after it.

Angry people get things done. Angry people start campaigns, organise peaceful protests, bring about social change. They raise awareness, write books, score goals, sing in rock bands, stand up and make people laugh… but they don't have to get aggressive and hurt other people. How do they do it?

How to get angry without getting mean

When something annoys you

First…

> Feel your anger.
>
> Don't deny it by saying you're hurt, fed up, confused, etc.
>
> Don't panic and lash out.

Feel the surge of energy and hold on to it. Some people say count to ten under your breath so that you can stay calm. I prefer to look around the room and name ten objects under my breath (*'one clock, two chair, three stain on the carpet...'*) because that gives you longer to steady yourself.

Then...

Express it.

This doesn't mean give someone a thrashing. The best way to express anger is simply to say you're angry – *'I'm angry that you moved my stuff'*, *'I'm angry that you took my crisps.'* You may not want to express it out loud, but say it to yourself. You need to know you're angry; you have a perfect right to be angry.

Finally...

Convert the energy into action.

This is usually a two-step process. When your anger first flares up your body wants action... now! You need to walk, run, thump pillows, kick a ball or listen to heavy rock music. (If Mad Mick and 'Six Pack' Parsons have chucked your school bag over the wall, running to get it will release some of the energy.)

When your body's calmed down, your anger settles to a slow burn. You're still angry, but you don't need to lash out any more. Your anger will give you the power and desire to work out a plan of action. (Are you going to tell on Mad Mick and 'Six Pack' Parsons because it isn't the first time? Are you going to let it go because it's a one-off and most of the time they're your mates? Are you going to get on with the rest of your life and not let their stupid games upset you?)

DON'T JUST GET MAD – GET EVEN!

That means don't waste all that lovely anger energy shouting and lashing out at people. Use it to understand what you want and work out how you're going to get it.

Some people never learn how to get angry without getting mean, and nobody gets it right all the time. Everyone sometimes lashes out when they're angry. When you get it wrong, don't beat yourself up about it (if you got mostly 1s in the "Are you A+ at anger?" quiz, someone else will probably have done that for you!). Apologise to anyone you shouldn't have taken it out on, put it down to experience and keep trying.

Kicking the cat

'Kicking the cat' is a technical term for when you're too scared to get angry with the person who's annoyed you (or possibly too sensible, if he's a headcase) so you take it out on someone else.

Here's how it works. Mum's had a hard day at work because her boss has been criticising everything she does. She can't argue with him in case she loses her job. She comes home fuming. You're lounging around watching TV, exactly the same as you do every afternoon, no sweat.

'Hi Mum. How was your day?'

Ominous silence. Then she lets rip.

'Get your feet off that cushion! Put your bag away! Don't leave that apple core lying around! Do your homework, get changed out of your uniform, tidy your bedroom!'

She really goes for it. Obviously it's not fair, but if you argue with her she'll make you do the washing-up as well, so you sort out the apple core etc. By the time you get back, you've missed the end of the programme and the cat's on the settee. Watch out cat!

A lot of people in the bs, bs and s-c fs situation take it out on their parents when they get home.

But taking it out on your parents is a v bad idea because you need them on your side. If you get stroppy at home, I mean more stroppy than usual (as you know, a degree of stroppiness is actually expected of you at your age), you'll end up with your parents on your back as well as the you-know-whats, and then you could collapse like the proverbial camel.

Look what happened to Conor.

Conor's story

Conor was having a hard time at school. Some new kid had decided it was clever to call him 'Specky Four Eyes' (yawn!) and now everyone was doing it, even his so-called friends. Well, he couldn't get cross with the whole school, so Conor took it out on his mum.

'I want contact lenses!' he demands, with much thrashing around and general bad temper. **'I need them! Right now!'**

'But you know we can't afford them,' she says, quite reasonably.

Conor does know that but he doesn't care. He makes his mum's life a misery, nagging and complaining all the time. He treads on his glasses so she has to get him a new pair. **'You might as well get contacts for me now,'** he says.

Obviously, Conor's mum doesn't like him bullying her all the time to get something she can't afford. Things get unpleasant. Now Conor has aggro at home as well as at school.

He gets new glasses (they really can't afford contacts), and guess what? His mum makes him pay something towards them from his pocket money. It's just the last straw!

When anger gets stuck

In fantasy land everything is nice and nobody gets cross. But in the real world bad stuff happens. People get angry, and they're right to get angry because if nobody gets angry, nobody sorts the bad stuff out.

If you don't let yourself feel angry with bullies, bigmouths and so-called friends

- they walk all over you

- you get exhausted with the effort of holding the anger in

- you get moody and unpredictable, because your pent-up anger is like a pan of pasta with the lid on that keeps boiling over

- you lose all your power and get depressed

- you can get ill, or have lots of accidents

- you get eaten up by resentment and bitterness

Some people never let themselves get angry, and most people bottle it sometimes. If you fall to bits when someone is nasty to you, don't beat yourself up about it (you've made yourself suffer enough!). Put it down to experience, and be ready for them next time.

Getting rid of old anger

Holding on to old anger keeps you locked in the past and wears you out. We say 'bearing a grudge' because a grudge is a burden. If you bear a grudge against someone it doesn't affect them in the least, but it weighs you down and saps your energy. One way to get rid of it is by forgiving.

Forgiving gets a bad press because it seems like a goody-goody weak thing to do. Actually it's very powerful. You could even see forgiving as a selfish act, because the person who benefits most is you.

Try it on something trivial first. Imagine your Dad forgot to get your football mag on his way home from work, and you've been in a sulk ever since (note that hasn't stopped him enjoying his TV programme and newspaper, but it has stopped you from enjoying anything at all).

You're past the pillow-thumping stage and you already know what you're going to do (i.e. pick the mag up yourself from now on) but you still feel cross. Get ready to forgive!

Forgiving

1   Remind yourself why you're forgiving him – so that you can let go of your grudge and enjoy the rest of the evening.

2   Write down on a piece of paper what you need to forgive him for (it may be more than one thing).

3   Read it through and feel your anger.

4   Let it go. It's in the past and it's keeping you there.

5   Say *'I have decided to forgive you and put what happened in the past where it belongs. I don't want anything from you and I don't wish you any harm. Now we are both free to get on with our lives. So be it.'*

6   Tear up the paper and get rid of it. For a small act of forgiveness, putting it in the bin will probably do. For a bigger one, you might prefer to bury it in the ground.

You can do exactly the same thing if you feel angry with yourself. There's no point holding on to it because who does that help? Acknowledge you got it wrong and let it go. Read the story of Miss Havisham and learn!

Miss Havisham –
a cautionary tale

Miss Havisham was stood up on her wedding day. When her husband-to-be (or not-to-be, as it turns out) didn't show up, she sat down in her wedding dress beside her wedding feast and refused to budge. She stayed there fuming for days, weeks, months and years, until her wedding dress went mouldy and her wedding feast was covered in cobwebs. Eventually the whole thing caught fire and she went up in flames.

Her husband-not-to-be probably never gave her another thought, so who was hurt by her world-beating grudge?

(Actually, several people besides herself were hurt – you can read about it in *Great Expectations* by Charles Dickens.)

Bullies, bigmouths and so-called friends are out of order. Be angry with them! But don't get carried away and lash out, or panic and fall apart. Feel the energy, hold the energy and use it to help you take whatever action you need to stay OK.

7 'What if I can't deal with it?'

Here is what everyone feels when they have a run-in with bullies, bigmouths and so-called friends...

Here is what everyone thinks...

'What if they don't stop?'

'What if it gets worse?'

'What if I can't deal with it?'

Sometimes, it all blows over quickly. Bullies and bigmouths find someone else to pick on, and your so-called friends start being nice to you again.

Then the fear shrivels up and dies.

But if it goes on, your worst fears seem to be coming true. They *aren't* stopping! It *is* getting worse! Before you know it, the fear has grown enormous, and you really can't handle it any more.

You pretend to be ill so that you won't have to go to school, or you start bunking off. You go miles out of your way to avoid your tormentors. You hide in shadows. You try to be invisible. You stop doing anything that might draw attention to yourself, like getting good grades or wearing new clothes. You stop being friends with anybody at all, in case you get shut out again.

If your enemies are armed, violent and dangerous, it's probably a good idea to avoid them (but not such a good idea as phoning the police). That's what fear is for – it keeps you safe.

But most bullies, bigmouths and so-called friends aren't into GBH, they just want to embarrass and humiliate you. Your monster fear is way out of proportion to the actual danger you are in. You don't need to give in to it in order to stay safe. You need to cut it down to size before it takes over your life.

FEAR

Cut it down to size.
Bin it!

Big fear, small comfort zone!

Fear doesn't feel nice, and mostly we avoid it by simply not doing things that scare us. That's called staying within our comfort zone.

the school bus

trying new recipes

answering in class

comfort zone

going in goal

going to the swimming pool

But when you have a problem with bullies, bigmouths and so-called friends your comfort zone can get very small.

Wearing new trainers

having a haircut

the school bus

trying new recipes

Coming top

answering in class

eating in public

getting a text

the dinner queue

going in goal

going to the swimming pool

changing for PE

looking at people

comfort zone

Then you have to face up to your fears and deal with them because your comfort zone isn't comfortable any more!

(A word of warning – always stay inside your common sense zone – don't try to blast through fear if it's warning you of actual physical danger.

The author will not be responsible for people overcoming their fear of stray rottweilers and getting chewed up!)

Cutting your fear down to size

Everyone knows that if you fall off a horse you should get back in the saddle as soon as possible. That's because when you've had a bad experience you fear it could happen again, and the sooner you face up to the fear the easier it is to get over it. The longer you put off facing up to fear, the bigger it grows.

By the time the fear's got bigger than you, there's no way you can tackle it head on. You have to work up to it in stages, starting with smaller fears first.

Aaaargh! Spiders!

Supposing you're scared of spiders (who isn't? I think they're aliens from a planet that I prefer not to imagine). If you see a spider in the house, you sit in the garden. If you see one in your bedroom, you sleep downstairs. If you see one in the bath, you panic and run out in your nothings.

(Note: the spider's got the run of the house and you're out in the cold.)

There's no way you could pick up a spider and put him out, right? Wrong! You can do it if you approach it in a step by step way. First do something spider-related you find a little bit scary. If you see a spider in a room, stay put. You know he isn't likely to come near you. You feel scared, but you can cope. This is called 'feeling the fear and doing it anyway'.

Now you know you can stay in the same room with a spider, you're ready to try something a bit scarier. Next time you see a spider, go closer and really look at him. It's spine-chilling... it's skin-tingling... but you know he probably won't come towards you, and you can do it.

Big adrenaline rush! Major triumph! By exposing yourself to fear, you are getting the experience of courage.

Now there's a spider in the bath. You want a bath. Is your fear going to stop you? You manage to stay in the room (you know you can do that),

and you manage to look at him (ditto). He's running up on to the window sill! You don't panic. You open the window. It would only take a quick flick, a moment's contact.

One sickening second of hairy spider on jelly-wobble hand, and you've done it! You've touched the spider, and put him out.

(Note: now you've got the run of the house and the spider's out in the cold. Result!)

Aaaargh!
So-called friends!

What works with spiders also works with so-called friends. Meet Hannah. She has a hard time with her friends because they are nice to her one minute and horrible the next. She's always walking on eggshells trying not to do anything to upset them.

Last time she got new trainers, they teased her for weeks. After the teasing died down, Hannah promised herself she would never go through that again. But now those trainers are old and falling to bits. Hannah's mum has bought her a new pair, but Hannah can't face wearing them to school. The new trainers are still in the box, Hannah's mum is annoyed, and Hannah's feet are always cold and soggy.

To build up her courage, Hannah practises by doing something she's a little bit afraid of, which is going to the corner shop. She usually avoids doing that because the shopkeeper, to prove how dim kids are these days, makes her work out for herself how much she owes him. She's afraid she'll get it wrong (which she usually does).

Now Hannah's faced up to a small fear and survived, she's feeling much braver. She's ready to wear her new trainers because although her bitchy friends might humiliate and embarrass her, she knows she can deal with that.

Note: there's often a good pay-off for facing up to fear.

Androcles and the great pay-off

Androcles was a Roman slave. His master took him on a trip to Africa to buy spices, and Androcles escaped. He was v pleased with himself, but then... he found himself face to face with an enormous lion!

After several minutes (or possibly years, Androcles couldn't tell) the lion still hadn't eaten him, so he picked himself up off the ground and opened his eyes. Then he noticed the lion had a big thorn stuck in its paw.

The lion looked so sorry for itself that Androcles went up to it and pulled out the thorn. Either the lion was grateful or it just wasn't peckish, it's hard to say, but anyway it let Androcles go.

Years later, Androcles returned to Rome to visit his friends. He was v pleased to be back, but then... he found himself face to face with his

old master! His master had him carted straight off to the arena because runaway slaves were always fed to the lions to put them off doing it again.

So Androcles was in the arena and they opened the cage and this huge lion came bounding out. After several minutes (or possibly years, Androcles couldn't tell) the lion still hadn't eaten him so he picked himself up off the ground and opened his eyes.

Guess what? It was the same lion Androcles had met before! It sat down in front of Androcles and purred like a pussy cat. The crowd gasped and the Emperor pardoned Androcles on the spot. He also gave Androcles the lion as a reward for being more entertaining than all the other slaves who just went out and got eaten.

Quite a pay-off for a few seconds of bravery!

Feel it ... and deal with it

You might find it hard at first to think of any small things you're afraid of. That's because we usually don't admit to ourselves that we're scared. We say, '*I know my limits*' and '*I don't see the point*'. '*I don't want to*', '*Why should I?*', and '*It's not my thing.*' We stop doing things that make us feel scared because feeling scared is uncomfortable.

So look at things you avoid doing, and ask yourself, '*Is it actually because I'm afraid?*' Here are some examples –

- '*I don't like going on the school bus. It's too crowded. I'd rather walk*' (and actually some boys once grabbed my bag and threw it around and I'm scared that could happen again)

- '*I don't put my hand up in English because it's not cool*' (and also I'm scared of looking a fool because our English teacher gets sarcastic if you're wrong)

- '*I don't like going in goal because it's boring*' (and also I'm scared the rest of the team will rip me apart if I let one in)

- *'I don't cook because that's girl stuff'* (and also I'm scared it won't work and my mum will get mad at me for wasting the ingredients)

- *'I don't go swimming any more on Saturdays because there are too many little kids at the pool'* (and also I'm scared I'll see Kelly's gang there again – last time I went they broke my hair brush)

Make a list of the things you don't like doing. Which ones are you avoiding through fear? Choose the least scary, and get started. It's as easy as that.

Five things that can help you face up to fear

Here are 5 things that can help you when you're ready to face up to fear.

1 Creative visualisation

(OK, it sounds airy-fairy, but don't skip this bit because it's good.)

A great way to build up your courage is by imagining being brave. (New research has found that you can also build up your strength and fitness by imagining you're doing exercise. Really!)

Don't say *'I'm not imaginative'* because everyone is. It's automatic. If I say I'm writing this on my laptop in a converted lighthouse with my dog beside me, you will automatically make a mental picture of me, the laptop, the lighthouse and the dog. The only difference with creative visualisation is you do it deliberately.

Here's a top visualisation for courage.

First, take a deep breath in through your nose and sigh it out through your mouth. Close your eyes, and take a few more deep breaths. Now think about a lion. He's coming across the hot African plains. The sky is clear and bright, the earth is red, the grasses are pale and dry. Feel the heat.

See the red earth. Smell the dry air. Hear the grasses rustle as the lion moves through them. Use all your senses as you imagine the scene.

Now be the lion. You're huge, you're fast and you're strong. No other animal would dare to attack you. If you want to, you can lie down right there in the open, roll on your back and go to sleep – you have absolutely nothing to be afraid of.

Feel how it feels to be a lion. Take your time. Enjoy it. Notice what happens to your body.

This visualisation makes you feel powerful and fearless. If you remember it when you're in a scary situation, it will bring those feelings back to you. If you do it often, you won't even have to conjure up the whole scene any more – you will think lion and feel fearless.

If lions don't do it for you, try visualising an elephant or giraffe, or any other animal that doesn't have to worry about getting gobbled up. Collect pictures of your animal and put them round your room. Your fearless animal will help to awaken the fearlessness in you.

2 Breathing

When you get scared, you either stop breathing or start to breathe very fast.

Notice your breathing. All you have to do is notice it, then it'll start to settle back to normal and you'll begin to feel more calm.

3 Lucky objects

Lots of people who work in scary jobs use lucky objects to help them. Actors coping with stage-fright, TV reporters working in battle zones, climbers and explorers alone in the wilderness – they all often carry a special object to give them courage. The novelist Graham Greene had to do research in some very dangerous places and he always carried his teddy in his overnight bag! I read about an actress the other day who never goes on stage unless she's wearing her lucky knickers (I hope she's got more than one pair!).

A lucky object is like a secret companion. It means you don't have to face your fears on your own, and that helps you feel braver and safe.

It's best to have a choice of lucky objects – then if you lose one you won't fall to pieces. Make a little collection of things that feel lucky to you. Here are some ideas –

• pebbles from your garden

- shells from a beach

- coloured tumble stones from a crystals shop. (People have always used semi-precious stones for courage and protection. These days you can get a pocket-sized piece of jasper, agate or tiger's eye for less than the cost of a cola)

- tiny model animals (I've got a collection of crocodiles I use if I'm meeting someone scary who thinks they can walk all over me!)

- brightly-coloured objects, like those yellow smiley faces

- things that make you smile, like rubber bendy dolls or figurines from your favourite cartoons

4 Now power

This is a common-sense approach to anxiety. If you're lying in bed worrying about what might happen at school tomorrow, you simply say *'Right now, I am safe. Nothing bad can happen. Right now it's OK to go to sleep.'*

Any time the bullies, bigmouths and so-called friends aren't around (which is most of the time), you can tell yourself, *'Right now, I am safe. It's OK to get on with what I want to do.'*

5 Keepers

This is like Now Power, but more imaginative. You name your worries and put them somewhere safe during the times when you know rationally that nothing bad can happen. You could give them to worry dolls, like kids in South America. If you haven't got any worry dolls, you can easily make some.

How to make a worry doll

1 Get a strip of soft, plain fabric.

2 Roll it up.

3 Tie it tightly round the top with some sewing cotton.

4 Tie it again a bit lower down.

5 Draw a face with a felt-tip or gel ink pen.

6 If you like, you can decorate the dress, or you can cut the dress part to make arms and legs by binding wool around them.

Keep your worry dolls by your bed and before you go to sleep, give one worry to each doll to look after. (If you've got thousands of worries you might need to select the top six or so – you don't want so many worry dolls you can't get into your bedroom!)

If you don't like the idea of worry dolls, you can simply shut your worries in a box. Like any ritual, this can actually be a very powerful thing to do. Try it. See how it feels.

Jonny's story

Jonny's French teacher, Mr d'Aggers (yes, really!), was the most mean man on the planet (or anyway in Latimer Road School). He loved making everyone's life a misery by setting tests they couldn't do and then ripping into them for being stupid.

Test day was Thursday. So every Wednesday evening Jonny did his best to swot up. He didn't get a wink of sleep because he was so worried, and consequently he was too tired in the morning to know which way was up, let alone the past participle of 'avoir'.

Jonny's little sister, Elinor, gave him her secret teapot. It was about the size of a ping-pong ball. She told him to put his worries in it when he went to bed, and get them out again in the morning (well, she was only 5).

Jonny humoured her. He found it worked! He slept really well and felt OK in the morning. He still got most of the test wrong, of course, but at least he hadn't wasted his time getting into a state.

Actually, a great and surprising thing happened after a few weeks. Mr d'Aggers was doing his usual tirade about how bad the test results were, when Elinor's teapot suddenly came into Jonny's mind.

Quick as a flash, he whipped off the lid and stuffed old d'Aggers inside. It was a moment of pure pleasure... though of course he got a detention for grinning in the middle of a telling-off.

Like I told you, Mr d'Aggers was pretty mean.

Make friends with fear

Bullies, bigmouths and so-called friends mean

You can try to avoid it by skipping school but those bullies, bigmouths and so-called friends aren't going anywhere.

Stop running away from fear because if you always run away from feeling fear you will never know how it feels to be brave. Build up your courage in a step by step way, by facing your smallest fears first.

When you learn how to feel the fear and deal with it, two great things happen. First, people stop being so aggressive towards you, because fear attracts aggression like a magnet attracts iron filings. And second, your life opens up because you have the courage to try new things, take chances, and go after what you want.

Make friends with fear. Get to know it and understand it. If you are in real danger it will keep you safe, and if you aren't it will teach you to be brave.

8 Goodbye bullies, bigmouths and so-called friends!

So here it is in a nutshell, the **Say Thumbs Up For Fun – End Misery! (STUFF-EM!)** method of dealing with bullies, bigmouths and so-called friends –

Start talking

Take response-ability

Be good to yourself

Hold on to the baby!

Don't let them grind you down

Make friends with fear

The beauty of the STUFF-EM! method is

1   It works

2 It's easy, because you practise on the easy bits of your life, like a boxer training at the gym – you build up real strength and confidence instead of having to pretend

But that isn't the best bit. Check out the line-up again. Ben's been working on the STUFF-EM! method. If you were looking for someone to pick on, would you still make a beeline for Ben?

So there you have it, the best bit of all – the better you get at dealing with bullies, bigmouths and so-called friends, the less you have to.

9 Wicked websites

www.childline.org.uk

Lots of useful information and true stories, plus
details on how to ring, text or write to ChildLine.

www.antibullying.net

Information about bullying plus plenty of sensible
advice from expert Andrew Mellor for readers
who send their problems to his Bully Box.

www.bullying.co.uk

Very clear, well laid-out website full of really
useful stuff, especially about cyber bullying.
Includes a 24-hour online helpline:
help@bullying.co.uk

www.jennyalexander.co.uk

If you'd like to find out more about me!

10 Here to help

There are several helplines you can call if you need to talk to someone. They're all completely confidential, so you can pour your heart out!

ChildLine Tel: 0800 1111   Lines are open 24:7
Text: 0800 400 222
Weekdays 9.30am–9.30pm
Weekends 9.30am–8pm
Calls to ChildLine are free and don't show up on itemised phone bills from landlines, 3, BT Mobile, Fresh, O2, Orange, TMobile, Virgin and Vodaphone.

Samaritans Tel: 08457 909090
Calls are charged at local rates
Email: jo@samaritans.org

Anti-Bullying Campaign Tel: 020 7378 1446

National Society for the Prevention of Cruelty to Children (NSPCC) Tel: 0808 800 5000

Index